EL GRECO

(DOMENICOS THEOTOCOPOULOS)

EL GRECO

TEXT BY

LEO BRONSTEIN

THAMES AND HUDSON

Frontispiece: *St. Luke*, Cathedral, Toledo

Originally published by Harry N. Abrams, Inc., New York

First published in Great Britain in 1991
by Thames and Hudson Ltd, London

This is a concise edition of Leo Bronstein's *El Greco*,
originally published in 1966.

Printed and bound in Japan

CONTENTS

EL GRECO

Δομήνικος Θεοτοκόπουλος

A FOREIGNER: Theotocopoulos the Greek was a foreigner all his life long. He was a foreigner in his own birthland, Crete: the luminous island, the proud torchbearer of fallen Byzantium, and since the seizure of 1204, humiliated, foreign to itself, the helpless subject of Venice. Foreigner he was when, young icon painter-artisan, he went (a little after 1560), like so many of his compatriots, to the still busy, still daring city of Venice, to live there, to work, to watch, and to absorb the great West at large. Foreigner he was in Rome, whither from the Venetian lagoons his adventurous will or some other urge more material directed him—from 1570 to 1576? or from 1570 to 1572 and then back to Venice again?—before his final exodus to Spain. And foreigner he remained in Spain, foreigner in Toledo, where he settled about the year 1577, and where he died April 4th, 1614. He was called El Griego —the Greek—by his Toledan co-citizens; in all the official documents, Dominico Theotocopuli (or Theotocopulo), Griego. Revealingly, he signed his pictures in Greek: Domenicos Theotocopoulos. And it was by the Italian form of his name, Dominico Greco (not even the Castilian form, Griego), that he is referred to in *El Arte de la Pintura*, by the painter scholar Francisco Pacheco, the Sevillian, who visited El Greco in 1611 and surely used the name by which the aged artist must have been known professionally.

Foreigner he was until the end, even beyond the end: a scarcely noticed foreigner-ghost, visitor-ghost of the following centuries; his very name, unknown in Crete, was also soon forgotten, if ever really retained, in Italy (the last trace of Greco's passage in Italy is the reference to him by Mancini, Pope Urban VIII's physician, about 1614). A puzzling foreigner-ghost he was to the nineteenth-century Romanticists, who were attracted by the aura of eccentricity: this legend of eccentricity, of madness even, having originated in the whispered slanders of Toledan sacristies of his time, and culminating in the twentieth-century "scientific" theories—now fully refuted—of El Greco's insanity, his astigmatism and other aberrations.

Not until our own age, conscience-torn and foreign to itself, was full and exalted citizenship given to him: in critical literature notably by Manuel Cossio's classical and unsurpassed work, *El Greco*, published in 1908; and more vitally, because couched in terms of Greco's own pictorial idiom, by Cézanne.

Here lies perhaps the secret of Greco's so often celebrated *españolismo*, his "Spanishness." It should not be called his, Greco's *españolismo;* nor "theirs," the *españolismo* of yesterday's Spaniards. It is really the *españolismo* of today's Spaniards, nostalgic foreigners to their own myth; it is they who have found in Greco, the Cretan, the sealbearer of their own citizenship.

And so, what is "ours"—his life's creations—should be clear and accessible to us; what is "theirs"—El Greco's life—should remain obscure and puzzling.

And obscure and puzzling his life is indeed. Was it as it is seen by the majority of modern apologists, for whom "nothing but the best" will do for Greco? Was it the life of a daring genius, whose inner prowess is joined to the expressive prowess of the mystical heroes and literary eagles of his age and of Spain? Whose external path is strewn with significant, aggressive, even arrogant happenings? According to these apologists, the external happenings are readily evoked and enumerated: Greco's early training in Candia, Crete (where he was born in 1541), under some famous master of icon-painting; his later studies in Venice under Titian, Tintoretto, and Bassano (the latter's controversial "second style" being partly due, some suppose, to Greco's collaboration); then Rome, where his arrogant challenge to Michelangelo's grandeur so aroused the protest of his colleagues that Greco was forced to leave. They tell us of his extravagant and luxurious existence in Spain, his financial success as a painter in Toledo, the house of sinister and illustrious memory—"nothing but the best"—the palace of the fifteenth-century sorcerer, Marqués de Villena, where Greco lived among his books of classical antiquity and Renaissance erudition; his mysterious and beautiful companion—"nothing but the best"—Doña Jeronima de las Cuevas (his wife? his concubine? a Venetian, a Toledan, a Cretan, a Jewess?)—the mother of his son, Jorge Manuel; the glamour and activity of his *atelier* (his busy collaborators, Jorge Manuel, Preboste, Luis Tristan); the glamorous friendships, surely with Gongora and Paravicino (who celebrated his genius in sonorous verses) and supposedly with Cervantes, Lope de Vega and all the other grandees of letters, of learning, and of elegance whom he would meet in the gardens and salons of Toledo; his frequent and victorious lawsuits....

Was this the way his life was? Worldly and triumphant?

Or would his life be the one we read from the numerous Toledan documents unearthed by El Greco's most earnest modern biographer, Don Francisco de Borja de San Roman, and from other testimonies as well? A gray life, of labor, of patience and trouble, vexed by outbursts of promptly retracted irritability; of financial difficulties and debts, of professional humiliations, even of yielding to the exigencies of commercialized art (his numerous replicas, many of them *atelier* works). A life of protracted lawsuits—not at all exceptional in the casuistic and torn world around him—where his work, submitted to money appraisal, became the prey of petty professional and church-versus-monastery rivalries, so typically Toledan. A gray life, of sickness perhaps (the right to represent him in all business and legal transactions, officially given by the ageing artist to his faithful servant and assistant, Preboste or Prevós, and subsequently to his son, Jorge Manuel, would argue for sickness). Yet it was probably also a life of studious quietness and domestic loyalties: his books, the music in his home, the many-roomed home that was left almost emptied of furniture at El Greco's death (the death of the poor); a life with Jeronima, the *persona de confianza y de buena conciencia* of his testament; then the friendship and protection of the good and modest Dr. Gregorio de Angulo; and, from the windows of his workroom, the eye's and heart's epoch-making view of Toledo, hemmed by the green river Tagus....

One does not know which life was Greco's. For, in the absence of documentary certainty, speculation is the only tool left for the work of scrutiny and criticism. The temptation remains to see a life of labor and worry, of intimacy—and of untouchable inspiration, too. But first and foremost, his was the life of a foreigner.

One is tempted thus to read in the symbols of his art, in its awareness, sensibility, and projected convictions, the meanings of the passion and the life of a foreigner: the longing for shelter and rest; the yielding to the solitude and to the brutality of the external; yet at the same time the finding of, and the withdrawal to, the one and only security—the intimate, the solidarity

1. El Greco. CORONATION OF THE VIRGIN. *Collection Max and Leola Epstein*

of togetherness, and the proud *"mas alto!"*—the "higher!"—of the poet.

In the whole of his slowly emancipated Spanish work there is the feeling of intense and silent communion, a plunging into one another's eyes, which, from the starry-night look on the Byzantine-Castilian faces of the *Burial of Count Orgaz* (page 63) to the chained glance between Christ and the confronting angel in the *Baptism* of Toledo (page 125), boldly triumphs over the much more obvious rhetoric of gesture. It is this intimacy and togetherness that makes his Holy Families into knots of fused solitude and solidarity. And the drama of El Greco's "winged hands"—the famous, universally exalted hands that are flames, birds, and banners—would this not be the symbolized drama of

a foreigner, the without-a-home traveler? The hands depart abruptly, they travel afar; they tear away from their living branches when they are many; when few they gather together, they come back and adhere all together to their common center; but when in solitude and separation—one hand pressed unctuously to the breast—they are lost, displaced, obedient, useless beauties, to be touched and themselves not touching. And do we not see the drama of a traveler also in the routes of his Toledos, ascending under the down-traveling skies, ascending and descending to meet in knots of unspeakable longing, to meet and to depart and to meet again?

Then there is the celebrated "realism" of El Greco. What is so unique in it, so peculiarly his, not Tinto-

13

retto's, not Bassano's, nor the North's maplike tracing of life's paths on the face of a man? It is the sudden coming upon us, the sudden emergence, of a face—its spatial nearness, its genuine familiarity, its averageness; and more striking yet is the insinuation of its nudity. El Greco, one is tempted to say, could be explained as the painter of nude faces—as the painter of the nude body, of nudity.

For very strangely, not only had this master of pious, reputedly mystical subjects and intentions painted so many nude bodies, but this nudity is not the idealized nude-clothed-with-nudity of the Renaissance order, but rather a crude, direct nudity of a medieval boldness.

Shall one conjecture that here too was a foreigner's rebellion or revenge? Perhaps. And perhaps, too, it is his inheritance from the Greek-Byzantine world of the austere human presence—suddenly confronted by the Renaissance cult of the beautiful nude. Above all, perhaps, it was his shock—rejection and attraction all at once—at this confrontation. For, in the later stages of his art—prefigured in the detail of the "Stoning"

2. THE PROPHET ZACHARIAS. Late 14th century(?).
Church of Brontochion, Mistra, Greece

on the hem of St. Stephen's robe in the *Burial of Count Orgaz* (page 35)—this nudity becomes, without losing its supremacy, a nudity that we embrace and reject all at once. It becomes more and more a new, hitherto unheard of, structure of El Greco's: a swift structuring of the proud human body in spiraling verticality; a rapid and passionate ascension of our touching hands all along its full sinuosity. With no obstacle to this touch—without anatomic accents of sex—El Greco's sexless, yet fleshy bodies impatiently spiral to their goal, that most precious of all things for El Greco, always different yet always the same: the human head.

This is not a mystical dematerialization, but rather an ultramaterialization: a concerted, vigilant working attention to the material craft problems of a painter.

El Greco's very typical strength transforms influences, direct or indirect, into plastic forms of his own. How much did he transform and distill from the Counter Reformation's new realism—all tenderness, sensuous directness, sanctification of the average, of the "already seen"? Tenderness: this great renewal of hope in the tired heart of an age, mobilized for power by the astute church of Loyola, now precariously triumphant over heresy.

How much of Tintoretto's poetry, how much of his forgotten street and room corners, his forgotten crowded lives coming out of nocturnal darkness to very sudden light—how much of all this has been transformed into Greco's structures? How much of Barocci's silvery radiance and bold, yet tender and average imagery? How much of these is in Greco's structures?

How much did Greco take from the realism of the art of the *bodegone*—that Spanish (and especially Sevillian) form of still-life painting, derivative, yet so different from its Northern and Italian models in its direct, unadorned bluntness? Would it not be the spirit of the *bodegone* which is transfused into Greco's realistic heads, making them *bodegone* heads with their sudden spatial nearness, familiarity, and bareness? And Greco's invention it is, too, not verbal or illustrative, but an invention of his hand, his eye, and his heart. *Invenzione*, in the narrative, secularized, and grandiose

sense demanded by the aesthetic lore of the late Renaissance, seemed to be Greco's special concern during
his Veneto-Roman and early Spanish periods (for
instance, his new themes of the *Cleansing of the Temple*,
of the *Healing of the Blind*, or of the *Espolio*). Yet in his
later periods it appears to become less and less his
special concern. Excepting, we may say, such real
inventions as his late *Laocoön* (page 121), or the *Vision
of St. John* (page 123), El Greco had, on the evidence,
yielded to the sanctimonious concepts and preferences
of his clerical Toledan clientele. In his growing indiffer-
ence to the verbal glamour, subtlety, and variety of
invenzione, can one read a foreigner's yielding before
the impact of the external—external in the social sense
—and a withdrawal to the shelter within? From the
rejection by the up-to-date Philip II of his striking
Martyrdom of St. Maurice (which might have been in-
spired by Carpaccio's *Ten Thousand Martyrs of Ararat*
in Venice) to the end of his life, El Greco did not cease
to retreat from the external and to withdraw to shelter
within, in defense and pride.

In Toledo, not the provocative, rich, and industrious
Toledo of the Imperial Court, but the now courtless
Toledo, crowded with hoods and their shadows, with
poor *hidalgos*, with beggars and with recent glories,
loved by the Orders, hated by the Curia and the
Crown, El Greco became the producer, useful and
popular, of imagery for people's devotions. Indeed,
when compared with Tintoretto's formidable *invenzione*, for instance, or with the Zuccari's or particularly with Pellegrino Tibaldi's subtle theologically in-
spired dramas (frescoed on the walls of the Escorial,
about 1588–96), compared with all such, El Greco's
subjects must have appeared to his contemporaries
(but not to us, who interfere in and complete his inventions) merely simple and devout ex-votos. Brilliant
to be sure, a little unusual and bizarre to be sure, in
their pictorial structure; but what did that matter, so
long as these images invited prayer and obedience?
And they undoubtedly gained him a commendable, if
humble, reputation in sacristies and monks' parlors,
but only a very slight one among the halls of grandees

3. THE PROPHET ELIJAH. 15th century.
Church of Peribleptos, Mistra, Greece

or coteries of the learned. Pacheco's failure to mention
the religious subjects of El Greco except once (in
praising him as the best and most popular painter of
St. Francis), at the same time that he speaks so profusely of the iconographic merits of the religious works
of all the major and the minor painters of the age, is
a striking and puzzling testimony of silence to this
point.

Yielding to the imposed external, perhaps in fatigue,
perhaps in sincere religious obedience, the foreigner,
"their" Greco, the Greco of yesterday's Spain, had
withdrawn to his inner shelter, his hand, his eye, and his
heart. And there he remained, hard and conscientious

4. ST. JOHN THE EVANGELIST. Circa 1100.
The Gospel Manuscript, Amiens, France

worker of his form, aloof yet fraternal to his own age, emerging into the future as the master of deformation: "our" Greco now, at last. But the "what" of the subject, the ex-voto and its contents, is "theirs," and with them remains. The form, El Greco's "how" and the sense of this form, is "ours," today's.

So much exalted and ultimate praise has been bestowed on El Greco: El Greco the pure mystic, the deformer of the body for the triumph of the flaming spirit; El Greco the pure Byzantine and the last; El Greco the Mannerist and the last; El Greco the pure Spaniard and the first one in art; El Greco the first Baroque painter and the pure one; and yet our first and pure astonish-

ment before El Greco remains unshaken. What principle and what passion, so obviously and in such accelerated intensity, both unite and separate the elements of his structure? There are the contrasts within his cool color scale as it enacts its assigned tonal plot simultaneously with his harmonic and centralized tone warmth, so typically Venetian: his all-honey canvases, or all-gray, or all-madder. And within his compositional schemes there are contrasts: the obvious armature of geometry—triangular, elliptical, concentric organizations of the picture planes—and at the same time, the presence of the irregular or unforeseen in it; the advancing, bulging volumes, and the flat contour ornaments, extended in profile.

What is this dual principle—above all this passion that it has, for many a work of the great masters expresses this same duality, but none possesses and is possessed by such a passion?

El Greco is all passion.

Almost all the themes of Greco's time could be found in his art: from G. P. Lomazzo's demand that the form should behave "like a live serpent when it moves" ("*Una serpe viva, quando cammina*"), to the poet Marini's bold declaration that "the only rule worth thinking of is to know how and when and where to break all rules"; from the Roman-Florentine tradition and theory of geometrized space, to the tendency, Venetian par excellence, toward total pictorial freedom (Dolce, Aretino, Pino); from the heroic blast of the late Roman Mannerists to the silent concentration and conscious modesty of a Barocci.

And how many more of those striking characteristics of the age we find reflected in Greco: the expression of intense melancholy, the *sensus dolorum* and, together with it, the mystical joy and curiosity about light permeating all, the *luce divina, lumo divino*, this great love of sixteenth-century thinkers. (Francesco Patrizzi's much-read *Nova de Universis Philosophia*, with its mystical theory of light as the explanation of all cosmic and spiritual development, was listed in El Greco's library in the first inventory made by his son after the painter's death.)

The intense interest in optics among the scientists of the sixteenth century, shared by the contemporary artists (among many examples that could be cited, Dürer's optical experiments in his drawings (figure 6) and Parmegianino's self-portrait with his abnormally enlarged hand seen in a convex mirror are particularly striking), must also have been El Greco's. It has even been suggested that the key to both the elongation and the convexity of Greco's figures is to be found in his scientific curiosity about optics, particularly about the laws of formation of images with the help of convex mirrors and lenses.

Equally intense was the interest of sixteenth-century artists in the rapid advance of mathematical thinking and practice. The end of the sixteenth century, indeed, already foreshadowed all the great advances of the full Baroque age: the boldness of analytic, descriptive, and, above all, projective geometry. This, too, was reflected in Greco. The planned consistency and complexity of the geometrical structure of his matured art has been noticed, if not proven, by modern students.

Even such a pictorial detail as the fallen figure seen from behind in a tormented anatomic position (page 93) was not Greco's invention, but can be easily found in the Italian art of his time, in the Zuccari among others.

The growing demand of the mature Renaissance for the emancipation of design from pre-established aesthetic rules (still so imposing at the end of the sixteenth century) Greco shared with his time very intensely. Gradually he built up his own freedom of contour, a freedom which is one of the aspects of his deformative tendencies and which was rather enhanced than inhibited by the underlying geometrical structure.

This may explain Greco's answer to the greatly displeased Pacheco, that "painting is not an art," meaning by that painting's liberation from artisan routine. It is here that it might be suggested, perhaps not irrelevantly, that just as in a certain sense any historical progress seems a coming into the foreground of something that has existed until then in the background, so

in the history of Renaissance painting one sees a certain freedom and sketchiness in the design of the background forms (for instance, in Botticelli and Filippino Lippi), emerging, during the later Renaissance, to prominence in the foreground in the principal figures. This emancipating shift affects the drawings (think of Leonardo's, Parmegianino's, or, later, of Barocci's innumerable and so highly emancipated, impressionistic drawings), as well as the very structure and technique of painting. Greco's sharing of this artistic inner change of his era might be one explanation for that extraordinary liberty of contour—sketchy, rapid, dramatic, a contour blurred here, accentuated there—which in his passionate application he pushed to the stage of systematic, conscious deformation.

Passionate application—that is the key. For it is the surprise in discovery and the passion and freshness in communicating it that makes Greco, the newcomer, so new and surprising in his art, so different from all

5. THE ASCENSION. 10th century. *MSS. the Benedictional of St. Aethelwold (Chatsworth Estates Company)*

others. And it was also the passion of a Byzantine, who by a centuries-long tradition, without, perhaps, being explicitly conscious of it, learned how to love and be loyal to patterns of thought and behavior, with the same passion, spontaneity and earnestness with which one loves what we call nature.

Traditionally, Byzantium as a culture is characterized by its passionate loyalty to the prototype of its Hellenic past, on all levels of its behavior. For brevity's sake, reducing the problem of pattern to its aesthetic aspect only, one could say that, in this tradition, Man and the perfection of his figure took precedence over everything else. In Hellas, the human figure absorbed all that in the visible world around it would complete it: skies, waters, summits; and this visible world was transcribed in symbols of human gesture and Man's limited body structure. Underlying this vision of Man's centrality and supremacy was the Greek idea that, like geometry's most ideal figure, the circle, Man was perfect in form. Byzantium—as well as the Renaissance later on—inherited this view: behind the Byzantium traditional formulation of space stands the Hellenic all-permeating concept of the stable, self-sufficient human form.

This does not mean that Byzantine art—nor for that matter the art of classical antiquity—was without genuine lyrical or dramatic content. All students of Byzantine art and especially of its late period (about the fourteenth to the sixteenth century) know how rich in invention and in lyrical freedom is this art, the art of the fourteenth-century Chora mosaics, of the fifteenth-century Mistra, and the sixteenth-century Mt. Athos frescoes, or the still more dramatic art of the Balkans and of the Slavic world.

Yet in its essential pictorial structure, in its conception of space, Byzantium—especially the later Byzantium of the Paleologi—was passionately attached to the pattern of organization that had been developed by classical antiquity. But, for reasons too long to explain, among which the infusion of Asiatic ornamental tradition was one of the most decisive, Byzantium transformed the classical pattern into a more complex configuration, more varied in plastic expression—a configuration that we might characterize as elliptical, or (having to do with the building of a volume in pictorial space) as ovoid. A Byzantine figure or group of figures, and also what surrounds it within a given frame, seems submitted to a kind of deformation with all the psychological expression of awe or terror that any deformation in art is bound to convey to us. (Is it not this which, in spite of all the tenderness and warmth of Greco's art, makes his deformations so disturbing?)

More often than not the Byzantine form appears to us as a terror-breathing form, bulging out, coming upon us, self-sufficient in its isolation from its surroundings (figure 2). Its significant symbolic elongation seems the very measure of the span from earth to heaven (figure 3). Above all, the Byzantine form is the symbol of Man conceived as an absolute, to whom the relatively stable world outside is subordinate. The most striking thing in late Byzantine representational dramas (and often in Greco, too) is the docility with which the plastic content of the space accompanies the protagonist in a choirlike repetition. Architecture, rocks, furniture, church symbols are cast into irregular-spheric, ellipsoid, or ovoid volumes, deformed for the sake of the central drama, and yield to the protagonist's psychological command.

It was the Byzantine tradition of loyalty to this

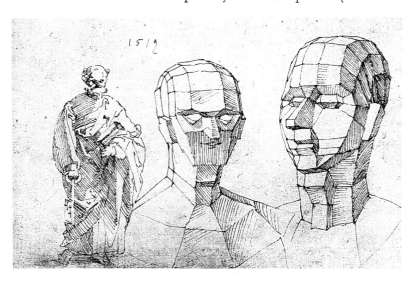

6. Dürer. STUDY OF HEADS.
Sächsische Landesbibliothek, Dresden

18

geometrical pattern of objects in space, rooted in Hellenic art, that must have made it easy for Greco to accept as familiar and ready for him one aspect of the art and aesthetics of the Western world, to which he came: the particular Renaissance predilection for the geometrical, which was Hellenic in origin and Byzantine by extension and perhaps by cultural contact. It is revealing to read in Lomazzo, so representative of his time, numerous passages, particularly in his *Idea del Tempio della Pittura* (1590), giving his credo of alliance between abstraction and expression, between geometry—the geometry of the sphere, especially—and art.

The Renaissance spatial structure with which Greco was confronted—the world to which Greco came with the Byzantine tradition—was based on a conflict not unknown in the Christian East, but which had there a different outcome. Greco as a newcomer was to feel so keenly and to embody so dramatically in his art this conflict between the Hellenic conception of the *static* human figure dominating the pictorial milieu and the opposite, the Western, principle of *mobile* interplay of figure and milieu, particularly evident in the Mannerist art of the sixteenth century, in which are renewed certain medieval conceptions of the figure.

In Romanesque art the figure becomes identified with its surrounding space. And it does so by torsion, a mobile presence at multiple points of contact with its frame—a dancing, spiraling, or suddenly rigid and elongated, compact, multi-axial or ubiquitous figure (figures 4 and 5).

Such is the world opposed to the world of Hellas.

Now, the Renaissance was the apex of both this conflict and the attempt to resolve it, that is, to fuse the Hellenic and the medieval elements. In this lies, perhaps, the essential character of the Renaissance, and also its distinction from the Byzantine aesthetic formula. It is this combination of two elements, the element of static presence of a milieu-dominating figure which goes back to classical antiquity, and the element of the dynamic figure-deforming pictorial milieu, that provides all the extraordinary complexity of the Renaissance artistic formula. Indeed, the fiery elements of

7. Dürer. CHRIST AMONG THE DOCTORS.
Collection Thyssen, Lugano, Switzerland

that conflict influenced each other. This influence—now juxtaposition, now fusion—of stability and mobility of forms is what accounts for the complexity of the Renaissance structure of volumes: spherical, elliptic, spiraling or cubistic (built on the principle of multiple crossing of planes), or expressively medieval still, mobile-ornamental.

Elliptic—almost Byzantine—is the deformed, elongated, and bulging volume of Pontormo's *Venus* (figure 8), with the menacing symbols of inhuman dramas embodied in masks—this sixteenth-century obsession; "cubistic," difficult, multi-axial, typically mannerist appear the spatial anxieties of Dürer (figure 6); both sphere and flat, isolated as a figure, but ornamental-continuous as a composition, is Dürer's spatial achievement (figure 7). And mobile-medieval is the sinuous contour of Simonetta Vespucci's grace, continued or echoed in the clouds around her (figure 9).

It is this new and tormented world that El Greco faced boldly and made his own. It is his exceptional vehemence and passion and lyricism in expressing the basic and grandiose drama of his time that makes him the Expressionist of the waning Renaissance.

19

8. Pontormo. VENUS AND CUPID. *Uffizi Gallery, Florence*

Here, another aspect of his art—another of those numerous keys to his "enigma," so eagerly looked for by his historians—could be suggested: the professional sincerity of a perfect and conscious craftsman. Greco does not use any tricks in his art. With sincerity and directness he introduces us to the intimacy of his procedures as a colorist: now adhesive fleshiness of impasto, now vibrating transparency of his superimposed, often contrasting layers of color, with the priming often untouched, bare, and his brushwork sometimes unhurried, smooth, uniform, sometimes nervous, rapid. And with the same sincerity and directness he *tells* us the stories he paints: he tells them to us visually in the very language of his craft. For instance, in the scene of his *Annunciation* (courtesy Wildenstein Gallery, N.Y.), Greco tells us textually the story of the Virgin's surprise and transformation: he makes Her face surprisingly deformed, asymmetric, and emphasizes this deep and personal transformation by contrasting its abnormality

with the plastic normality of the angel. And this is how he tells us the story of the Virgin's exaltation in the *Assumption* of San Vicente (page 127). In the *Holy Family* of Madrid (page 83), the story of the Great Tempest—Christ's mission and death—is transmitted to us as spectators of the picture and as witnesses of the event through the vortex-like body of the little St. John the Precursor.

In the *Baptism of Christ* (page 125) he paints an event that, with its prophetic vision and impact, fills not only the life of earth but that of heaven. And he tells us the fulfillment of this event textually, not only by fusing, or mixing the two worlds—earth with its baptism, heaven with its glory—but by painting the fullness of heaven and earth. The linear continuity and interaction of forms, the *horror vacui*, that seems to reign there, conveys to us better than words could do the precise feeling of fullness and total achievement, which is the real subject matter of the picture.

At the end of his life, El Greco was commissioned to paint a portrait of Cardinal Tavera, who had died in 1545. He painted it from a mortuary mask—and he painted this mask faithfully, as he saw it. But he opened —resuscitated—the eyes of the dead man's stony face, and he gave us the most living eyes he had ever painted (page 103).

From Pacheco we know that Greco used suspended wax and clay figurines for his composition and grouping of figures, and perhaps even for the modeling of the individual figures. From the attitudes and bold foreshortenings of these dolls, which seemed to come to life under the flickering light of candles, he tried to guess all the possible attitudes of living bodies. This procedure, which probably goes back to Dürer, he learned from Tintoretto, who used it profusely.

Sometimes, when El Greco wished to communicate a certain feeling, conveyed to him by the subject, he must have painted, one surmises, these dolls as he saw them, exactly, textually, with all the strangeness of the artificial, the mechanical, the different-from-the-living, about them. The sudden infusion of the mechanical aspect in a figure, often accentuated by the contrasting and intensified "naturalism" of another figure or figures near it, is one of the most striking features of Greco's style. Such for example is the figure of the Christ Child accompanying St. Joseph (page 67), with its puppet-like head and arms as if added to, or segregated from, the body; or the figure of the Infant in the scenes of the *Holy Family* (pages 73 and 83), with its cut-out aspect and its doll-like, mechanical flatness and articulation, contrasting with the rounded natural volume of the Virgin's beautiful head and hands, and accentuated by the outlining dark shadow-like zones around the Infant's silhouette.

To return to El Greco as a narrator, we may say that he tells us the stories he paints, sincerely and directly, without tricks or literary-verbal complexities of interpretation. In this, too, El Greco reveals his time. For the Renaissance was not, as it is often considered to be, the era of artistic thought par excellence, as opposed to the intellectual-philosophical. Not at all. It was,

indeed, an era in the history of man's thought when the deepest moral-philosophical thinking was fully expressed in terms of visual symbols which were more subtle, more complex and daring than the verbal symbols were or could have been. It was not the Platonists—a Marsilio Ficino, or a Castiglione—not even the influential Leone Ebreo, all verbalizing heroes of the Renaissance *élite*, who had then deepened philosophy's perspective; but Michelangelo, a Leonardo, a Dürer, a Tintoretto, the aged Titian, or the aged Greco. Pacheco praises Greco as a "great philosopher" who wrote much and well on art, but no trace of his writings has reached us. Greco's philosophical greatness and wisdom were the greatness and wisdom of his craft as a painter.

And so El Greco the Byzantine, coming into this time, discovered the Man, the New Man for him. He understood—and so did all the great ones of the age— that the Man in it was the emancipated, proud,

9. Piero di Cosimo. PORTRAIT OF SIMONETTA VESPUCCI
Musée Condé, Chantilly

Promethean artist. He accepted this as the very definition of the soul of Man, not only the Man of his time, but of all times.

He had guessed it already, perhaps, in his native and Italianized Candia, but it was in Venice that he must have discovered the New Man. It was in this Man's company that among the familiar pictorial visions of St. Mark's Byzantine interior he listened to the new music of a Gabrieli, a Willaert, a Zarlino; he watched the unquiet, religious, and inventive spirit of Tintoretto reaching with the ease and grandeur of a rare genius the two extremes of his space construction: the one "cubist," cutting diagonally, enigmatic, flat-ornamental in its elements, full, voluminous in its results (figure 11); the other much easier but more lyrical and energetic in its galloping depth (figure 10).

He never forgot the boldness of Tintoretto's space, in which the moral *terribilità* of both figure and milieu in their plastic interrelation was enhanced and ex-

plained. And he never forgot Titian's deep craftsman's love of a surface-and-color continuum, which was Titian's expression of life's continuum as he saw it. But the great revelation of Rome and Michelangelo had yet to come, and it was not so much the message of Michelangelo the painter as it was the message of Michelangelo the sculptor. Now, it is not so much sculpture's narrative content as painting's that usually lends itself to purer verbal representations. By inhibitions or revolt, Michelangelo made his paintings into lofty and powerful verbalized sculptures; and he introduced into his unfinished sculpture all the *sfumato* and sinuosity of a Leonardo, all the fleshiness and penetrating adhesion of a pictorial substance, all the medieval dynamics of interaction, and all the drama of geometry's far-reaching concepts. "That the form be pyramidal, serpentine, multiplied by one, by two, by three" ("... *multiplicata per uno, per due e per tre*"), Michelangelo said toward the end of his life to his

10. Tintoretto. LAST SUPPER. *San Giorgio Maggiore, Venice*

22

11. Tintoretto. SUSANNAH AND THE ELDERS. *Kunsthistorisches Museum, Vienna*

pupil Marco di Siena. And this became his message to his century. One thing is obvious as we look at Greco's early, Italian productions: the young Byzantine, in constant astonishment before the Italian miracle, seems to have forgotten his old world of Mistra, of Athos, of Candia, and to have turned resolutely to the New Man and his craftsmanship. But this he could not master as yet. All the works of his Italian period that have come to us reveal his dramatic effort and failure to understand correctly the new (for him) rules of spatial depth and illusion in a picture; of correct placing of figures and of their actions; of solid balancings and proportions. This failure accounts for the inaccuracies (so ingeniously shown by T. F. Willumsen) of his *Healing of the Blind*, of his two early versions of the *Cleansing of the Temple*, and of other works.

The revelation of Rome made his failure clear to him. The failure was there, and so, under the shock of this awareness, he made his decision. Back to the origins, back to Byzantium, back to the armature and the older geometrized pattern of space. And suddenly, in well-merited compensation for this anguish, everything became clear to him. The irregular, ovoid volumes of Byzantium; the "cubistic," dramatic, multiplaned space of the sixteenth-century Mannerists; and the medieval vision of the dynamic, ubiquitous figure; all this, and its goal, a new and comprehensive idiom for man's lyrical-moral self-expression, became clear to El Greco.

Illuminating and practicable became Michelangelo's command. Serpentine, spiraling, thus ubiquitous ("that the form be . . . multiplied . . .") became to him not only the pictorial line but the planes and their oblique self-crossing, the mannerist volume itself; serpentine, the whole pictorial universe: figure, milieu, colors, lights, shadows, all became one interrelated, vibrating

23

12. Berruguete. GIDEON. *Cathedral, Toledo*

symbol of the visual emancipation of Greco's New Man—of Greco, himself, of his vision and expression. The secret of his destiny was thus revealed to him. And this is, perhaps, the whole secret of his art too.

Yet, at that stage, it was only a dream and an inspiration. The realization came later—slowly, gradually, painstakingly. It had started on the eve of his exodus to Spain: perhaps with works like his bold, multi-axial, and tumultuous new version of the *Cleansing of the Temple* (page 55), several times later repeated, but once only, toward the end of his life, improved again (the *Cleansing*, in the Church of St. Ginès,

Madrid). But it was Spain that allowed him to withdraw into his Michelangelesque revelation and to become there finally the watcher of his own liberty. For Spain left him free. Spain, so much in love with the verbal, had not yet begun to care about the emancipation of the visual. And so El Greco in his secret Toledan withdrawal could fully profit from the silent permission around him to be free, as a painter. But something else was granted to him there, as well. Great was his joy, and great the influence on his decisions, when, on his arrival in the haughty and impoverished city of Toledo, he found, unexpectedly, a real companion in struggle: Alonso Berruguete, a sculptor again, Michelangelo's pupil, one of the eagles of the Spanish Renaissance. (Greco found not the man but his work, for Berruguete died in 1561, sixteen years before the Byzantine's arrival in Toledo.) Berruguete understood, and expressed boldly, Michelangelo's torment and order (figures 12 and 13). His work, containing the innermost meaning of torment and order, became also the very expression of the Renaissance's maturity.

And this maturity, one could say, was the passage from the grandiose, heroic, and self-satisfied conception of man, to a humbler, but more responsible, because less satisfied conception of the later sixteenth century. It was also the passage from the earlier Renaissance man's impulsive acceptance, observation, and admiration of the surrounding world, to an attitude of meditation, absorption, and doubt—a passage comparable to the psychological transition from *looking* to *seeing*.

The Man of the waning Renaissance was the inner man who *sees*. Berruguete's *Christ* (figure 14) is the projection in art of this inner *seeing* into the expressive rhetoric of the figure and its milieu. With no world there but tormented Apostles around Him, Christ is all attention, interrogation, lyricism, and deepest *seeing*.

The discovery of Berruguete's work must have been the great joy of El Greco's life. And so, one imagines, the completed permission to be free, to form and deform and form again, was there all about him, in this fiery land of Spain where both freedom and oppression have always been consumed and reborn together.

Thus, El Greco's march toward the final realization started: a silent, untiring, obstinate march. The final goal was there, in all its clarity and passion: that man should become one with the world; that he should know it, should *see* it, and should testify to it. Indeed, the inner subject of El Greco's art is the seeing, the knowing, and the testifying to, a miracle: the miracle of a body emerging from another body or from the milieu, the miracle of adhesion and interpenetration, of levitation or self-liberation.

El Greco's march was painstaking. His first great ensemble in Spain, the Santo Domingo retable (pages 48 and 53), already bears the mark of his decision. Then, at almost the same time, came the next step, the flaming *Espolio* (page 57) and, towering over this period of trial, perhaps over all the forthcoming periods, the troubling masterpiece, *The Martyrdom of St. Maurice*. In the burning coolness of its Byzantine color scale and organization—the dominant yellows and blues, the silver luminosity of the all-permeating gray; in the startling separation and, at the same time, juxtaposition of the isolated, proud figure, and the spiraling composition (figure 16), El Greco found the explanation both of his trial and his goal. Separate, but separate to unite; unite, but unite to reunite still more!—this was his battlecry. Then, after the worldly failure of *St. Maurice*, came the great withdrawal and another masterpiece, the serene masterpiece of the *seeing* inner man: *Orgaz*. A great battle was over, the goal now very near. The higher he ascended, the more exalted, but also transforming —deformative, rather—became the memory of his ancestors: the Byzantine ellipse of isolated volumes, the medieval "serpentine" continuum. A passionate urge to unite these two, to fuse them, was the urge that presided over El Greco's space-building. Asymmetric, ovoid (Byzantine) is the space of the *Coronation of the Virgin* (figure 1) and of the *Immaculate Conception* (figure 15); continuous, ornamental (medieval)—the adhesion there of the form, of the figure, to this geo-

13. Berruguete. JOB. *Cathedral, Toledo*

metric frame. And not only asymmetric, ovoid, and continuous-ornamental in its volume, but also in the now contrasting, now harmonious color accord; in the suddenness (very late Byzantine) of the high light's action, in the "deformed" anatomy of bodies, faces, hands. El Greco's art, the art of the flame that deforms, of conflict, of discomfort, of alternating despair and serenity, became more and more toward the end of this march the art of joy and security and ease—the joy, security, and ease of a craftsman, master finally of all his means.

It was also the joy and security of the rebel poet, Shelley:

14. Berruguete. CHRIST. *Church of the Saviour, Ubeda, Spain*

15. El Greco. IMMACULATE CONCEPTION.
Collection Thyssen, Lugano, Switzerland

To defy Power, which seems omnipotent;
. . . to hope till Hope creates
From its own wreck the thing it contemplates.

It was the ease of the great goal reached: his last dream of the Virgin's *Assumption* (page 127), *"mas alto!"*—"higher!" But no further did he go from there: Death and Resurrection, Ascension and Descent of the Holy Spirit—all themes given to him and his art from the outside world—became one integrated theme in his inner world.

And here comes a question—not from the historian, who knows there can be no answer to it—but from the wonder of a spectator: What is the particular theme—the icon or image—that El Greco would have chosen and taken with him in his withdrawal, as his own *invenzione?* One wonders: A face, a man's face, would it not be that? An *Ecce Homo's* face—the *Ecce Homo* of Greco's time, the time of melancholy, of death and hope coming out of despair, the time of *"mas alto!"* too? A face of the new *Poverello*—a new face of St. Francis? One wonders.... Indeed, was not El Greco famous for his numerous icons of St. Francis (figures 17, 18, and 19)—this emaciated, angular, sharp-nosed, obliquely projected profile, the profile of an average *bodegone* face, too? Certainly El Greco was second to none as the painter of St. Francis, said the very orthodox Pacheco.

Was not St. Francis Candia's adopted and beloved saint? The ancestor of Renaissance emancipation?

And then one wonders again.... Is it possible that this icon, so cherished by the Byzantine in his Toledan withdrawal, was transformed, when the urge to transform seized him so strongly, into a disguised image? What, after all, is the real subject matter of the mysterious *Vision of St. John* (page 123), the strangest of all El Greco's creations, at the end of his life? Who is the emaciated, angular, sharp-nosed, and so sharply projected adolescent—androgyne and angel without wings—kneeling yet advancing toward us, inundating us with the awe of his nearness, so terrible and so fragile? Who is he, his arms and body a screaming invocation;

16. El Greco. THE MARTYRDOM OF ST. MAURICE. *The Escorial, Madrid*

17. El Greco. ST. FRANCIS RECEIVING THE STIGMATA
WITH BROTHER RUFINO. *Hospital de Mujeres, Cadiz, Spain*

18. El Greco. ST. FRANCIS.
Museum of San Vicente, Toledo

the meager one who unites heaven and earth, hope and despair, despair and the *"mas alto!"* and who brings to life the flaming, spiraling, pale, and beautiful nudes of the dead? Who is he?

A deeply rooted medieval Franciscan tradition in the West—a secret tradition of the poor artisan—wanted the *Poverello* Saint to be the opener of an Apocalyptic Seal—the opener of a new and liberated life given to all whom the old life had oppressed. Did El Greco know this? Did he paint in that picture, perhaps without knowing that he really did so—his true image of St. Francis—the secret of his heart? One wonders....

19. El Greco. HEAD OF ST. FRANCIS.
Hispanic Society of America, New York

DETAILS OF COLORPLATES

NOTE:

For additional commentaries on the paintings
in this section, please refer to the Colorplate section.

FIGURE 20

CLEANSING OF THE TEMPLE
(detail of Colorplate 4)

Painted 1584–94 (Cossio); after 1604 (Mayer)
National Gallery, London

The money-changers, panic-stricken more by the sudden revelation of power in the suave Christ than by the punishment itself, try to escape, but they cannot.

Brilliant is the planned confusion of this detail. The upward-catapulted figures, beginning with the one at right, make a frantic—explosive—series, away from the Christ and diagonally back into the picture space. Counteracting this upward straining into the depths of the picture is a falling series of horizontals which advances diagonally downward and forward to the very surface of the canvas at the left: the bent arm of the same standing man who begins the first series, the strong yellow edge of his garment, then the arm of the woman below, and the back of the downward-reaching figure in the corner.

All of this action and counteraction, advance and recession, very exactly conveys to us the impossibility of escape.

FIGURE 21

EL ESPOLIO (detail of Colorplate 5)

Painted 1579 (?)
Cathedral, Toledo

The eyes of the three women are upon the wood where is being prepared the place for the nail that will pierce Christ's foot.

Christ's foot: has ever living flesh been more convincingly given in art? The living, pulsating, healthy flesh is presently to be pierced, nailed through, emptied of life and blood.

But the hand of the Magdalen, made of the same flesh, is nevertheless alien to the sacrifice: its soft beauty, enshrined against the dark background of the Virgin's robe, isolates from the tragedy the Magdalen, whose young and robust figure is clothed in lovely colors of distant hills and ripened fields—the colors also of the man who is so completely engrossed in his task.

Such is the impetus and intensity of this moment of women's watching that there is no available element of pictorial expressiveness left inactive here. The main color themes—the shining ocher, the blue, and the reflected, pale wine-red—cross each other and meet boldly as stigmas of wrath in the very figure of the man who prepares the wood of Crucifixion.

Facing this wood and the condemned, sacred flesh is Greco's torn and crumpled signature: Greco's wrath and Greco's distress and, one should add, Greco's passionate urge to convince. For no one had ever been more strongly dominated by this urge—the very urge of his time—than El Greco.

FIGURE 22

BURIAL OF COUNT ORGAZ
(detail of Colorplate 8)

Painted 1586
Church of Santo Tomé, Toledo

Death, so El Greco tells us, is simply the descent into the elemental and primeval quiet.

The scene of the burial is such a descent: a melodious convergence of quiet and concentric curves descending toward the final quiet of their last and deepest curve; the dead, yet so relaxed, body of the knight in shiny armor, flanked by the triumphal fanfares—gold and red—of the attending saints.

Two beautiful and festive hands—lost butterflies of surviving vanity—palpitate between pomp and grayness before flying away forever.

The face of the man looking at us from above St. Stephen's adolescent head is supposed by some writers to be El Greco's self-portrait.

FIGURE 23

BURIAL OF COUNT ORGAZ
(detail of Colorplate 8)

Painted 1586
Church of Santo Tomé, Toledo

The ascension of the dead grandee's soul is a tremendous and difficult affair. At the left-center, the still shapeless baby soul, a chrysalis (in Gómez-Moreno's happy expression), carried by an angel, has to cross many a sinuous road of heaven's approach before reaching the deep heart of the Celestial Rose where Christ, the Judge, presides over the choir of angels and saints, with the Virgin and John the Baptist below, at His right and His left.

What dictates the structure of this upper half of the *Orgaz* composition is no longer the lower half's quiet and harmonic curves, but the strident rushing of oblique edges, crossing or completing each other; the screwlike forms, as in the figure of the soul-carrying angel; and the forward-thrusting clouds and mobile, angular limbs. It is a strikingly medieval ornamental structure in its interlaced system.

In spite of the joys of heaven's *Gloria*—the white radiance of Christ, the intense red-and-blue of the Virgin, the *allegro* of the little angel astride a cloud in so grand a manner; in spite of this joy, the tragic sweep of congealed clouds—heaven's supporting roads—and the biting sharpness of gray and yellow lights maintain all the solemnity and *terribilità* of a never-again repeated Day of Judgment.

FIGURE 24

ST. JOSEPH AND THE CHILD
(detail of Colorplate 10)

Painted 1599–1602 (Mayer)
Museum of San Vicente, Toledo

St. Joseph's cast-down eyes express a sad tenderness and love. And so heaven had sent down to him—in a great, headlong rush—the loveliest creatures it had formed, to inspire and, perhaps, to convince him: the loveliest childhood and adolescence, the loveliest flowers, and the loveliest rhythms of clouds.

FIGURE 25

VIRGIN WITH SANTA INÉS AND SANTA TECLA (detail of Colorplate 11)

Painted 1597–99

National Gallery of Art, Washington, D.C. (Widener Collection)

Pure arabesque of wreathlike, arrayed hands—how can this cool ornamental play of color, line, and shapes convey to us the meaning of human solidarity? Yet it can: an atmosphere of seriousness, melancholy, and loneliness, clothed with hues of gold, of silver, and of roses, radiates from the faces and the compact, living heaven to the hands—and there infuses them with exaltation and appointed meaning.

FIGURE 26

ST. MARTIN AND THE BEGGAR
(detail of Colorplate 12)

Painted 1597–99 (Mayer)
National Gallery of Art, Washington, D.C. (Widener Collection)

St. Martin is about to divide his ample green cloak with the beggar by cutting it in half with his sword.

El Greco exalted and revived the waning ideal of medieval spirituality: the ideal of the divine and thus unbounded generosity incarnate in the Christian knight. This was the very ideal that Cervantes, Greco's exact contemporary, was then rescuing so heroically from abuse and secular confusion.

A few direct, personal, and transparent symbols suffice for Greco's rendering. At the left, the hands giving and taking, the folds of the sacrificed cloak, the sword's hilt: a complex, embroiled focus—a symbol of the world of human charity, a world so complex and difficult because still so human. At the right, the immaculate and intense beauty of the white horse's head symbolizes a world still indifferent to the drama of charity, an animal world humanized and made sublime here by virtue of its sheer beauty.

Between these two worlds, as if joining or relating them to each other, is the unsheathed sword held in readiness for the act of charity. And soaring high in the blue-and-white serenity of the sky, towering over these symbols, is the head of the young knight: a haughty and detached, yet sweet and melancholy adolescent head, both symbol and embodiment of the fullness of Christian spirituality.

FIGURE 27

FRAY HORTENSIO FELIX PARAVICINO
(detail of Colorplate 21)

Painted 1604–9 (Cossio)
Museum of Fine Arts, Boston

The shadows here are a rapid juxtaposition and crisscrossing of minute color trails: of most delicate lights and deepest greenish-black darkness.

Where this occurs with most intensity—around the eyes, the nostrils, the temples—the resulting vibration of luminous particles extends into the larger, even zones of color, freed from darkness: the middle of the forehead, the cheeks, the nose. The luminosity of these zones becomes so enhanced as to give the entire face the quality of a substance never seen, never touched, before—palpitating, phosphorescent.

The thick flow of darkness around this face—the beard, the hair—makes a sacred shrine where the opaline stone of the poet's face is guarded.

COLORPLATES

ASSUMPTION OF THE VIRGIN

Painted 1577

158 × 90"

The Art Institute of Chicago

This *Assumption* belongs to an ensemble of eight canvases painted by El Greco for the high altar of the newly rebuilt conventional Church of Santo Domingo el Antiguo. The picture is dated 1577; this is a rare and happy circumstance, for it fixes the date of El Greco's establishment in Toledo. The architecture and decorative carvings of the retable were executed by Juan Bautista Monegro, the sculptor, after Greco's sketches.

Confronted by the mature craftsmanship—in design, modeling, coloring—which is displayed in this earliest known work of Greco's Spanish period, we are faced with the persistent question: What previous steps in his artistic development could have led the Byzantine to such a mastery of his craft?

The *Assumption* shows undeniable traces of Italian influences. But the subject, treated so dramatically by Titian, Tintoretto, and Veronese, is given here a very unusual character of quietness, of silence, one would say.

Quiet is the Madonna's ascension; quiet the witnessing of the miracle by the Apostles. Already there appears in this picture one of the main themes of Greco's future art: the theme of witnessing, the sharing of, and testifying to, a vision. The Apostles do not show us—the spectators—their astonishment or ecstasy. They attest, they explain to each other the meaning of the miracle and of their witnessing of it.

ASSUMPTION OF THE VIRGIN (detail)

Painted 1577
The Art Institute of Chicago

Had Greco, before coming to Spain, already painted large and complete canvases, even frescoes, in Italy—as Willumsen tries to persuade us? Was he so busy with orders while in Rome that he had to take a collaborator, the talented Lottancio Bonasti, probably his pupil? Nothing is known for sure. The researches and discoveries of R. Pallucchini and others seem only to reaffirm the fact of young Greco's intense curiosity and variety of experimentation.

To prove, if such proof be still necessary, El Greco's mastery as a realist when he first arrived in Spain, this group of heads, as well as the details of the large figure seen from the back, should amply suffice.

More striking, however, than this realism is the presence already of one of those distortions, so typical of Greco's later works. This is the head of the young man facing us—but not looking at us—from behind the figure standing with its back to us. It is undoubtedly a portrait. Its importance in the picture is obvious. And to emphasize its importance, El Greco did not shrink from reversing—or at least from giving us the illusion of reversing—the accepted laws of perspective: the face is not only presented as if detached or cut out from somewhere else and then placed where it is now, but it seems as if it were nearer to us than the head of the Apostle behind which it is really situated.

HOLY TRINITY

Painted 1577–78
118⅛ × 70½"
The Prado Museum, Madrid

The influence of Michelangelo, Dürer, or Taddeo Zuccaro is usually evoked with respect to the conception and the composition of this canvas—one of the set painted for the retable of Santo Domingo el Antiguo—as well as to the attitudes and the anatomy of the figures. More impressive and certain than this borrowing, however real and instrumental it may have been, is the impact of El Greco's creative will, which makes this work already so personal and so mature.

One particular aspect of El Greco's pictorial genius is revealed here with special care. This is the feeling of adhesion, of the figure's continuity with the substance, as it were, of another figure or of the surrounding milieu.

This feeling, which was later to become the all-permeating aesthetic and psychological force of El Greco's art, is given here still in its early stage of expression, touching only small portions of the picture's field. It is present in the tightly fastened bunch of cherubs' heads at the foot of the dead Christ, the toes of his foot, the sole of the angel facing Christ, the half-visible hand of the Father supporting his Son's body. Technically, this remarkable pictorial success is attained by opposing minute zones of high lights—almost splashes of light—to the dark and thick outlines closely surrounding them.

A feeling of grayness—cadaverous and ashy—floats above the entire scale of colors and seems even to subdue the glitter of golden luminosity which inundates all the forms. As if in contrast to the exuberant robustness of the anatomies, El Greco seems to have wished to convey to us, through the voice of this gloomy gray, the sense of present death—of the dead Body mourned in front of us.

CLEANSING OF THE TEMPLE

Painted 1584–94 (Cossio); after 1604 (Mayer)
41½ × 50½"
National Gallery, London

El Greco often painted the same subject several times. In this picture we have perhaps the best of his late versions of a subject which he originally painted in his still-transitional Italian period. The subject of the Saviour driving the money-changers from the Temple is one of the rare themes that could satisfy the Protestant as well as the Catholic world of that time; for both the Reformation and Counter Reformation were officially aiming at the purification of the Christian Church.

Many elements here are still Italian-Venetian. But striking are the marked reduction of depth in the active crowd, the Byzantine ellipsoidal, bulging volume of the figure of Christ, the interrelation of sharp angles and curves in the drawing of single figures, the continuity of line from figure to figure across the picture plane.

Greco's real contribution is in the approach to the problem of constructing space with many opposed axes. Two main directions cross each other: one, stable and balanced, is parallel to the picture plane and the background wall; the other, oblique, is projected diagonally from the purposely accentuated head of the bent-over figure on the lower left of the foreground, the head bending toward us drawing us into the picture.

Whatever crudity of experiment this abstract armature of space might reveal to us, it is mitigated, harmonized, in the strict musical sense, by the *a cappella* vocal arrangement of colors: the now contrasted, now combined yellows, blues, greens, and grays gravitating around, and reflecting in suave and discreet halftones, the central melody of blended blue and madder—the purplish figure of Christ.

EL ESPOLIO

Painted 1579 (?)
112¼ × 68⅛"
Cathedral, Toledo

As a masterpiece it was already hailed by Alejo de Montoya, the Toledan gold-smith and arbiter in Greco's litigation with the Chapter of the Cathedral; and this praise decided the issue of remuneration in Greco's favor.

The *Espolio* shines like a most precious jewel. The burning ruby of Christ's robe consumes the cool tonalities that gravitate around this flame—the gray, the ocher, the blue and violet—and creates a hitherto unseen splendor: the com-plementary blue shadow on the yellowish surcoat of the bent figure, the intense reflections of red on the gray-violet of the knight's armor.

But, just as in the *Cleansing of the Temple*, it is the spatial organization that is intended to convey visually the psychological theme—here, the divestment of Christ on Calvary. The tunic, its presence and integrity, is the reality here. But this reality, as we know it, is going to be destroyed, divided among the soldiers. And the story of this impending drama is given in the very drama of the space. Around the powerful axis of Christ's figure a compact volume-sphere of realistic heads is constructed and is advancing on us. Below is the second level of spatial activity: the intersecting planes (in the modeling and the positions of the three Marys and of the soldier that prepares the wood) create a restless, Mannerist, "cubistic" space. The two levels are not merely juxtaposed, they interpenetrate; and the very uneasiness of this separation communicates to us the drama of anxiety and divine release.

ST. JEROME AS A CARDINAL

Painted 1571–76 (Cossio); last period (Mayer)
23 × 18½"
National Gallery, London

The span in dating is revealing; Cossio puts this picture in El Greco's Italian period, while Mayer places it amongst the later works. The *Cardinal* is a stylistic puzzle: Italy is there, and so, very obviously, is Byzantium.

The elongated and upthrust triangle which encloses the entire silhouette is in striking opposition to the downward convergence of the beard and the folds of the mantle. Yet, in vivid contrast to the absolute and abstract linear geometry of the effigy stands the freedom of its character as a portrait.

Awe-inspiring and distant is this image—the image of the Church's power itself, one would say. How removed from each other—and from us—are the active hands and the proud head! Yet see how joined they are in intimate effort to meet: the floating heavy beard is lengthened in order to span the separating zone of the red mantle.

This *St. Jerome* of El Greco is not the *terribilità* of the Church. This is a Cardinal who does not want to be a Cardinal, even as Jerome did not want to be.

An inscription—apocryphal—appears in the margin of the book nearest the Saint's body, and some have accepted it as an identification of the actual subject. It reads: "L. Cornaro, Aet. Suae 100. 1566" (L. Cornaro, in the year of his life, 100. 1566).

A LADY

Painted 1594–1604 (Cossio); 1578–81 (Mayer)
15¾ × 13"
John G. Johnson Collection, Philadelphia Museum of Art

Doña Jeronima de las Cuevas, El Greco's mysterious life companion—is this her portrait?

With colors to paint joy, flowers, jewels, early youth (here, the enamel-like radiance of the skin; the transparency of the modeling shadows; the luster of green and purple seen through the veil, the Cretan veil; the all-orange hue, suggestive of petals and gold)—and with a brush so fine and precise (details of the lips, the eyelids, the nostril) as to remind us of a precious and festive Persian miniature, El Greco, nevertheless, had painted the melancholy of a woman's aging face.

The poetic intention of this contrast instantly lends its meaning of restrained sorrow, sweetness, and inevitability, inscribed on this still very beautiful face, to all the other elements of opposition that went into the building of this image: the luminous head and veil welded together into one elongated, irregularly outlined ovoid, and isolated completely and enigmatically from the dark background; the quiet and regular horizontality of the features of the face, enigmatically also upset, as if cut through, by the diagonal and restless planes of the veil.

How little quiet is this quiet face!

Even the great divergence in the dating of this work by Cossio and Mayer (a divergence that occurs with regard to several others, equally puzzling, of El Greco's creations) adds its note of perplexity to the enigma of this portrait.

However, one should suggest here that stylistically the earlier date, 1578–81, is more acceptable. The jewel-like aspect of the color presentation and a certain linearity in the structure of the shapes evoke Greco's earlier works, even the works of his Italian period.

But then, if one accepts that date, could this aging woman be the beloved companion of El Greco?

BURIAL OF COUNT ORGAZ

Painted 1586
191⅞ × 141¾"
Church of Santo Tomé, Toledo

"My sublime work," El Greco himself called this painting, in a court proceeding. Yet humbly and obediently he had but painted here a story commissioned by the parish priest of Santo Tomé.

A long inscription below the huge picture (and interrupting it there) tells us this story: Two-and-a-half centuries earlier, at the passing away of the pious Lord of Orgaz, Don Gonzales Ruiz, the dead knight was honored at this Church of Santo Tomé, amidst assembled nobles and clerics, by the descent from open heaven of St. Stephen and St. Augustine, who themselves lifted the body and put it in its sepulcher.

The artist was asked to paint this miracle, and he painted it as he saw it: as the witnessing of a miracle. A little boy (Greco's son, perhaps) introduces himself and us to the event.

The faces are so silent, the hands so telling. Below, the rhythms are quiet, undulant; above, a swirling vortex. The nearness of so much happening. Everything here belongs to the psychological world of witnessing.

Is it the juxtaposition of two worlds that is painted here—heaven and earth; pictorial richness and privation; warmth of tonality and coolness of color contrasts; solitary figures and consolidated forms? Is it conciliation or conflict? Silence. And is the radiant beauty, melancholy, and kindness of all these men's faces a deep memory of ancient Greece? Or is it Greco's rejection of all violence in life—above all the violence of death, the execution and destruction of beautiful faces and beautiful bodies too often seen by him there, in Toledo, when victims of the Inquisition were executed?

Yes, that is what it must have been.

MAN WITH HIS HAND ON HIS BREAST

Painted 1577–84 (Cossio); 1578–80 (Mayer)
31⅞ × 26"
The Prado Museum, Madrid

Whose portrait is this pyramidally silhouetted, perhaps too painstakingly constructed, effigy of a haughty and sweet, melancholy and vain, Spanish nobleman? No one knows. The ethnic type could be interpreted as typically Castilian, or as beautifully Byzantine. What is clear is that this portrait belongs to the same world of quiet, melodious, and elegantly purposive portraits as the *Burial of Count Orgaz* (page 63). Here, too, it is not so much the originality of pictorial-psychological invention that counts, as a certain forcible and very conscious expression of a definite Grecoesque purpose. Indeed, this work's most dramatic technique of throwing into relief the illuminated face and hands against a very dark background is not El Greco's: it is Venetian—Tintoretto's, Titian's, above all. So also is the affected and insistent position of the hand on the breast, as if in obedience to the injunction, both humble and self-satisfying, of Ignatius Loyola: "Each time you fall into sin, put your hand to your breast while grieving that you have fallen."

And even the intense expression of all the subtle contrasts of dark and light, of the showy and discreet, the realistic and abstract, that entered into the making of this portrait is indubitably Venetian, too.

What is El Greco's own is the very awareness, the consciousness of this intensity, its integrity, and unfailing presence. The clear presence of this category of intensity—at once exaltation and meditation—is what appears to be El Greco's greatest gift to us. The airiness, as Cossio says, and the impasto technique of this portrait—a little too carefully worked (the preciosity of the lace ruffs, of the delicately wrought hilt)—point to the early Spanish period of the master.

ST. JOSEPH AND THE CHILD

Painted 1599–1602 (Mayer)
44½ × 22½"
Museum of San Vicente, Toledo

St. Joseph, the husband of the Virgin and foster father of the Child, is leaving the country where he dwelt till now. The reason for his leaving is perhaps given in the keen poetry of El Greco's questioning itself.

Why is there so much tender sadness in the attitudes of the Saint and the Child; why, in return, so much impetuous joy in the sky around the Saint's head? Is it in compensation for the Saint's merits, or in redemption of some wrong done or to be done to him that flowers are poured on him from heaven? And why is the frightened Child clinging so tightly to Joseph, as if seeking protection (or offering it)? It is a serious Child, his head and the immoderately long arm, as if for eloquence's sake, almost segregated from the body—as if added to it in a puppet-like fashion.

Far, far away already, under the low horizon, lies the unlikely Toledo, perhaps the wrong-doing city; far away from the traveling Saint's hand holding the staff is the other end of this staff, joined to the already traversed landscape behind him.

Though there are many unanswered questions, the guiding theme that gives cohesion to this work is, in Greco's usual and earnest way, not hidden to us. It is given in the pictorial structure itself. A poignant world of solitude and solidarity, bound together, is the real and guiding theme of this painting, one of Greco's most touching. A deep, somberly gray world, where the figures are continued in, completed by, their own environment: the ornamental radiation of their outlines into the arabesque outlines of clouds, of wings, and of Toledo.

VIRGIN WITH SANTA INÉS AND SANTA TECLA

Painted 1597–99

76⅛ × 40½"

National Gallery of Art, Washington, D.C. (Widener Collection)

Colored splashes of minute shadows, bluish-green, gray-violet, brownish, and pure silver-gray, tensely cluster around zones of pure, even, flowing light; winged heads of cherubs protecting the Virgin's feet; bulging, transparent clouds, with vague, floating objects in them, half covering the two worshiping angels; delicacy of zigzagging whites, fringing veils and curls; mellow modeling of the Virgin's head—all the newly emerged, so Italian world of emancipated design and coloring is present here and duly transformed by Greco's style, his liberty. No work of his middle period could better reveal than this one all the professional skill of a great colorist, as well as the expressiveness of his geometrical schemes. Nowhere, indeed, is Greco's major theme of the body's elevation more geometrically evident than here, in the repetition of two angles, one emerging from the other, formed by the space between the two saints and the Virgin's blue and madder draperies. How convincing and actual becomes, by this token, the great event of the body's self-lifting!

ST. MARTIN AND THE BEGGAR

Painted 1597–99 (Mayer)
75⅛ × 38⅝"
National Gallery of Art, Washington, D.C. (Widener Collection)

To be familiar with what we call miraculous, to be astonished with what is familiar, was always the sign of a true mystic. In this sense, El Greco was a mystic. He painted miracles without astonishment, and he painted what was most familiar to him—man's body and its proud, upward rush—with astonishment and passion.

In this scene of a knight sharing his cloak with a beggar, the significant contrast between St. Martin's complete attire and the beggar's complete nudity is like a ritual sacrifice to another, greater, all embracing nudity: the enhanced nudity of the beggar, the nudity of the white steed in its hallucinating nearness and humanness, the nudity of the radiant, immense sky. To this lovable sacrifice a song of pure and abstract tonalities, of unmixed blue, white, green, and black, is consecrated. And love is its subject. From the paired legs of the legendary man and the legendary horse to the paired eyes of the two youths and thence to the paired beauties of sky and heads, we rapidly descend to the very center of Greco's passion: the emerald green of a lowered landscape into whose flesh the white flesh of the lifted foreleg plunges. And there we remain, too, not in a plunge, but as if fixed in this most lovable spot of Greco's poetry and vision.

HOLY FAMILY
(VIRGIN OF THE GOOD MILK)

Painted 1594–1604 (Cossio); 1590–98 (Mayer)
44⅛ × 41⅜″
Hospital of San Juan Bautista, Toledo

This picture comes from the same source of tenderness and serenity that brought forth El Greco's works in the Chapel of San José; and it has the same loneliness and passion that we feel in *St. Martin and the Beggar* (page 71), *St. Joseph and the Child* (page 67), and the *Virgin with Santa Inés and Santa Tecla* (page 69).

The sentimentality in the faces of the Virgin, St. Joseph, and St. Anne does not clash with the modern preference for restraint upon effusion in art. Such is the intensity of the sentimental themes here—meditation, solidarity, compassion (the healing hand on the Child's head)—that it could only in part be revealed. It is in part discreetly concealed behind the formal language itself: the solidarity and tenderness of the wreath of hands, the wreath of invisible flowers and angels protecting the Child; the solidarity and tenderness of the cloudy sky that opens its blue joy to protect the Mother.

A passionate hue of honey and roses makes the colors here still more penetrating.

ST. LOUIS, KING OF FRANCE

Painted 1586–94 (?)
46 × 37⅜"
The Louvre, Paris

A king? What an awkward and indecorous way for so famous a monarch, knight of the Catholic militant sainthood, to display—while being dressed—all the insignia of his majesty: the *main de justice* lifted by a half-denuded arm; the scepter nonchalantly lowered, as if neglected; the heavy crown ill-becoming the head of this tired, but strong, man. As though to accentuate all this, El Greco has introduced a page boy, robust and purposeful.

A saint? Nothing is here to denote the presence, visible or invisible, of sanctity; nothing if not the slightly pathetic awkwardness, the feeling of stage costume and unwanted pomp—even slightly ridiculous—which is heightened by the nakedness of the arm, but contrasts sharply with the intense genuineness of the face.

The pictorial treatment is frank and direct. As though to heighten the enigma of the representation, the brushwork is smooth, the textures and surfaces are beautifully rendered, and the drawing is precise and deliberate.

CHRIST ON THE CROSS

Painted 1590–1600 (Cossio); c. 1580 (Mayer)
98½ × 70⅞"
The Louvre, Paris

This canvas was painted about the same time and in the same mood as the *St. Louis, King of France* (page 75). Unctuous is the piety of the two correctly portrayed donors in healthy prayer; unctuous is the beauty of the healthy, well-fed, splendidly portrayed body which Greco here uses to represent Christ; patient and delicate the accuracy of the flesh modeling and the polish of the color.

But from behind all this easy reverence comes the prophetic anger of the steel-edged, mourning clouds. They hang from the arms of the Cross in heavy, swirling masses; they envelop and flatten the figures with their load of voluminous threat. The showy self-righteousness and security of the figures is disturbed. They are not securely placed any more: they are floating fragments of superficial exaltation, on the ocean of a portentous and truly exalting sky.

The light flaming here and there, streaking the edges of the Cross, is of great beauty and invention.

AN UNKNOWN MAN

Painted 1584–94 (Cossio); 1594–1600 (Mayer)
18⅛ × 16⅞"
The Prado Museum, Madrid

One can see many visitors at the Prado standing before this modest-looking portrait, in longer contemplation than before any other of the master portraits of Greco. The "unknown man" is not at all unknown to them. We are pleased and astonished to meet him here; we know him living somewhere, not far from us, exactly the same unknown as evoked here by the painter. He might be a *hidalgo*, poor or not, he might be a saint, past or present. But above all, he is a good man, a kind man. He is El Greco's man. For El Greco had always been in search of a good man's face. Good or bad, he painted man's face as good—and never a better man's face, never a kinder man's face than this one.

How did he succeed in telling us this? Chosen and contrasted qualities are undeniably there: the finesse and attractive symmetry of the features—so aristocratic, as we commonly say—but also, in contrast and combination, a certain boyish sloppiness in the faint disorder of the hair, the moustache, the asymmetrically pointed beard; then the contrast between the wide-open, light-colored eyes, and the dark, thick eyebrows, lifted high, as if to make still more astonished, childlike, and innocent-looking the eyes of the middle-aged man.

Yet none of these expressive contrasts—and no matter how many more are added to them—could convey to us, when summed up, the precise explanation we are looking for. It is not so much in these contrasts themselves as in their mitigation that El Greco's success seems to lie. Two technical procedures could be mentioned as helping to accomplish it: first, the extreme delicacy and variety in the dark-to-light modeling, and the obvious emphasis on the smoothness of the brushwork; secondly, the general impression of a monochrome tonality that seems to submerge and bring together, and thus mitigate, all the opposites.

It is as if Greco were saying to us: always contrasts—true life is nothing but contrasts; but truer to life, and truer than life, is the mitigation, the redeeming of contrasts. For that is what the best and truest in life—the face of a good man—looks like.

CHRIST BEARING THE CROSS

Painted 1594–1604 (Cossio); 1587–92 (Mayer)
42½ × 34⅝"
The Prado Museum, Madrid

What, from the first, distinguishes the puritanism of the southern Counter Reformation from that of the northern Protestant Reformation, is that the Catholic temple-purifying, temple-strengthening authoritarian rigidity was partly submerged or concealed by the tremendously popular and fluid stratum of pious emotionalism. Ignatius Loyola's *Exercises* reflect this most successfully. The anxiety-stricken and at the same time sophisticated Catholic humanity found a temporary respite, a psychological vacation, in the very exaggeration and primitiveness of this sentimentality.

Thus, El Greco's image of Christ bearing the Cross, extravagant as it might be for modern taste in its honeyed, comfortably pious, and dramatized sentimentality, must have had a totally different effect on those of El Greco's contemporaries in Toledo—then so influenced by Levitical and Jesuit thought—for whom this icon was made.

El Greco's Christ is perfection complete: the image of perfect humanity. Nothing can be said against this image—thus nothing about it. It does not touch anything and nothing can touch it. It can only be shown or revealed—revealed by itself.

Perfect and dramatic are the eyes of El Greco's Christ—and the precious, overemphasized tears in them. Perfect and dramatic, the virility of his head, his neck, and his robust shoulders. And perfect also and dramatic the feminine beauty of his hands. The tapering fingers of the right hand are without any blemish of any activity on them. The affected bend of the left hand's little finger is simply a gratuitous condescension of its grace. The hands that are going to be disfigured on the Cross do not touch the Cross, do not touch anything. They should not be touched either. They are shown to us—they reveal themselves to us—in their passive beauty. (Indeed, although this canvas is generally known under the title of *Christ Bearing the Cross*, it would be more appropriate to name the subject *Christ Embracing the Cross*.)

A golden, crepuscular warmth of Venetian colors and light adds more sentimental sweetness to the Saviour's figure.

HOLY FAMILY

Painted 1594–1604 (Cossio); 1597–1601 (Mayer)
42⅛ × 27⅛"
The Prado Museum, Madrid

Toledo was full of distressed and suppliant refugees from the oppressed Greek lands. They had hastened to Spain in search of help, financial help mainly, for their relatives and friends held captive by the Turks. In the last years of the sixteenth century and the first years of the seventeenth, El Greco and especially his relative (brother?), Manusso Theotocopuli, who was then living in Greco's home, took an active part in the rescue campaign. One can easily imagine the artist's home resounding with lamentations and narratives of cruelties inflicted on his compatriots. Greco's work must have reflected this distress which he shared. Indeed, the first years of the seventeenth century were also the first years of El Greco's intensified distortions, increasing the torment and storm in his figures and compositions.

This *Holy Family* belongs to this period and to this mood. With the tempest approaching, the small Family is gathered very close together in contemplation and protection of the naked Child. The little John the Precursor is prophesying, and his body has already become the center of a cosmic whirlwind; the veil over the Virgin's reflective face is swelled out with the wind of fear.

ST. JOHN THE EVANGELIST

Painted 1594–1604 (Cossio); 1600–1604 (Mayer)
35¼ × 30⅜"
The Prado Museum, Madrid

According to legend, when St. John the Evangelist was in Rome, the Emperor
Domitian tried to kill him by poisoning the Sacramental Cup. But the poison
turned into a serpent which saved the Evangelist and his companions, and killed
his enemies.

In Greco's painting, the Saint seems to be explaining to someone not visible
to us the mystery of Christian faith and spiritual truth. Conviction shines from
his young and touching face, and he displays the heavy chalice of sacrifice and
redemption and the fabulous serpent that issued from it. The tangible symbol
and its miracle become the convincing and final proof.

Indeed, it is not the Saint whom Greco is painting here, nor the symbol, nor
the miracle. What he is really painting is the proving, itself.

That is why the hand pointing to the chalice is given such an excessive and
emphatic length, and the other hand seems to be identified with the chalice which
it holds. The five fingers, repeating the five circular steps at the base of the chalice,
become part of the symbol itself.

DON FERNANDO NIÑO DE GUEVARA

Painted 1596–1604 (Cossio); 1596–1600 (Mayer)
67½ × 42½"
The Metropolitan Museum of Art, New York

"There isn't an atom of charity in these pupils," says the writer, Arturo Serrano Plaja. An easy statement and an easy deduction: there it is, a portrait of the Great Inquisitor; therefore, he must be heartless—and so on.

But El Greco's heart and hand were in search—always in search—of a "good man's" image. And so, if this man was lacking charity, El Greco gave it to him. The magnificent portrait of the Cardinal-Inquisitor is not an image of pomp and rigid authority, but one of insecurity.

The Inquisitor is seated as if he were flying (the oval delineation of the lower part of the robe), and this insecurity of position is enhanced by the security—the plastic aggressiveness—of the bright sheet of paper signed with the artist's full name in Greek. The left half of the grand figure is so strangely and obviously tormented or stormy, while the right one is given so much repose; the left hand's fingers are distorted, as if pulled violently toward the right, and the folds of the robe are also pulled—very rigidly—in the same direction. His head is framed neither by the wall, nor by the door, but placed in-between.

The face is of magnificent workmanship; a sad and intelligent face (the refined, sensitive, palpitating nose)—the intelligent sadness of a Semitic face. The glance seems to us rude and inquisitive, pulled to the right also. But this glance is insecure. Take away the spectacles—and the velvety eyes of a kind man will appear, with the gift of El Greco in them: charity.

FRAY HORTENSIO FELIX PARAVICINO

Painted 1604–9 (Cossio)
43¼ × 33"
Museum of Fine Arts, Boston

Blood red is the silence that here seals up the too-ardent, perhaps too-dangerous lips. Red (in Byzantine fashion) is the outline of the sensual fingers.

Paravicino is the perfect contrary of Niño de Guevara (page 87). If the Inquisitor is the image of insecurity, Paravicino, the poet-preacher of the Trinitarian order, is the image of security. The glance of the Inquisitor is both fixed (on us) and hidden; Paravicino's burning eyes face us openly and freely, but they reach and secure something beyond us. And if the folds of the Cardinal's purple are rigidly pulled away, here all the folds of the spectacular dress are displayed, and fall softly with ampleness and freedom of movement.

Paravicino's left hand holding the books is not pushed or pulled away as is the Cardinal's, but is itself pushing, pulling away, one could say; in any event, it secures the gliding balance of the scholarly folio with the small volume, probably of verse, upon it. The luminous pallor of the poet's face is as ardent and frank in its expression of laboriously secured convictions as is his left hand's voluptuous penetration into the flesh of the little book, and the other hand's showy grace.

Paravicino was a scholar and a poet, as well as a glamorous royal preacher at the Court of Philip III—an erudite professor at Salamanca at the age of 21, a monk rising to high posts in his order, a subtle disciple of Gongora. In four crystal-hard and crystal-brilliant sonnets he celebrated the genius of El Greco, and in one of them told how a bolt of lightning—allegorical, one guesses—traversed the artist's studio one day without causing any damage.

FRAY HORTENSIO FELIX PARAVICINO
(detail)

Painted 1604-9 (Cossio)
Museum of Fine Arts, Boston

How would a Titian paint this hand? By dissolving the tips of the sensuous fingers into the sensuous shadows of what surrounds them. The exalted beauty of the hand would be included in the beauty of the entire figure and in that of the outside world. But the strict individuality of the hand would, probably, be dissolved too.

El Greco's vision of reality is different. He did not dissolve the contour of these fingers; he accentuated, in various ways, the outlines of each.

What he dissolved or, rather, sacrificed, to the truth of the form-shaping light, is the detail inside the outlines. Thus the individuality of the hand—the hand of Paravicino—is preserved. With the general, universal sense of tactile and visual consistency, the sense of luminous reality of an object in space is satisfied too.

Had Velázquez seen and admired this hand?

RESURRECTION

Painted 1584–94 (Cossio); 1603 (Mayer)
108¼ × 50"
The Prado Museum, Madrid

This painting is marked by the boldness so characteristic of El Greco's last period. Thus, a later date, c. 1608–10, seems to be more likely than Cossio's 1584–94.

The theme is the major theme of Greco's art: the witnessing of the body's levitation: this self-liberation of the body offers the sole tangible proof of the spirit's victory over matter, as this mystical concept would be expressed in verbal and naïve terms.

The witnesses in El Greco share in the progression of the event. The downward pull of the fallen soldier's formidable weight impedes the not less formidable upward rush of the other soldiers; this creates such an outburst of anxiety and escape among the bodies that, in order to prevent the destruction of all, a dynamic outlet had to be found.

The outlet exists in the almost intangible push—a push expressed by the void between the tip of the foot and the tip of the flagstaff—given to the newly created young body of Christ. A miraculous, yet natural, ascension of this luminous new body is achieved. The disorder of bodies in turmoil below becomes an accompanying support; the equilibrium of rhythm is re-established, and with it the continuity and interconnection of subject and pattern.

ST. DOMINIC

Painted 1604–14 (Cossio); 1603–5 (Mayer)
39 × 21⅝"
Museum of San Vicente, Toledo

Gone from the face of such an inexorable saint as this St. Dominic is the great sweetness of El Greco's *Poverello*! For in Greco's world, St. Francis, the father of spirit's humility, is the very expression of passionate giving. In Greco's many paintings of St. Francis the gift of meditation shines from the saint's face into the surrounding penumbra. Here it is the opposite expression—the expression of passionate taking—that defines the image of St. Dominic, the father of spirit's pride and wealth, in ardent prayer.

The figure of the Saint, his face framed by the hood, the white at the edge of this hood, and the folds of the robe are made of the very same matter and the very same forms as the obedient surroundings: here we have the geometry of sudden flashings of light—so Byzantine!—the awe of a sky void of earth, coming from dark to light.

ST. BERNARDINO OF SIENA

Painted 1604–14 (Cossio); 1603 (Mayer)
106 × 56¾"
Greco Museum, Toledo

St. Bernardino of Siena, feeling that episcopal power ill-suited his life as a Franciscan, had refused three bishoprics. He died in 1444. In this painting El Greco erected a monument to the Saint's refusal.

Bernardino is painted very erect and quiet, and at his feet stand three miters, symbolizing the three bishoprics. There is as much distance from the delicate, bare feet of the Saint to his delicate bare head as there is from the miters to the sky above. But the sky is joined to the humble earth by the marvelous, upright, and continued growth of the human figure, while the sky is separated forever from the pointed, rigid miters which, being symbols, no longer have growth.

SELF-PORTRAIT (?)

Painted 1584–1604 (Cossio); 1605–9 (Mayer)

23¼ × 18¼"

The Metropolitan Museum of Art, New York

Most writers on Greco consider this the master's self-portrait. The second inventory of El Greco's effects made by his son, Jorge Manuel, and dated August 7, 1621, mentions a portrait of his father ("*un retrato de mi padre*"). In 1926, Mayer claimed that this painting was the portrait mentioned in the inventory.

The portrait is of an old, sickly, and tired-looking man; perhaps, as Cossio has suggested, he is suffering from the tertian ague. It is remarkable how the unusual grayed tonality of the face—the pigment of an ashy, yet luminous texture—expresses the decay, the almost cadaverous decomposition of the flesh.

Yet this decay is painted with the certainty of a geometrical absolute. The linear geometry of the structure is emphasized not only in the accented oval of the head, but also in the elongation, the triangulation, of this oval, which connects it with the triangles of the ears and the fur collar.

The face of this elderly man appears in several of El Greco's paintings; particularly resembling it is the *St. Luke* reproduced as our frontispiece. According to legend, St. Luke was the first Christian to paint the Virgin and Child, and numerous artists (Ribalta, for example) had represented themselves under the name of their patron saint. It is tempting to accept the theory that in this image of St. Luke we have the most faithful portrait of El Greco. The individuality of this passionate and oriental face is unmistakable. It is also tempting to think that the slight strabismus, or crossing, of the eyes would, by self-projection, account for the presence of the same deviation in so many of El Greco's people.

According to both Cossio and Mayer, the *Self-Portrait* and *St. Luke* were painted during approximately the same period of Greco's life, yet the disparity in age between the two faces is evident. Our acceptance of either or both of these paintings as a portrait of Greço is at best a hopeful guess; mystified by the obscure facts of his life we desperately wish to convince ourselves that we have at least an image of the man.

PORTRAIT OF JERONIMO DE CEVALLOS

Painted 1604–14 (Cossio); 1608–12 (Mayer)
25⅛ × 21⅜"
The Prado Museum, Madrid

El Greco, as we have seen, became a passionate and responsive interpreter of the liberation of painting, chiefly the liberation of color and light by the sixteenth-century Venetians. Sufficient for us to consider this painting of Jeronimo de Cevallos, jurist and author of works on law and politics: it is perhaps the richest and most revealing of all of Greco's late portraits.

But the simultaneous use of all the liberated means of pictorial expression—color, light, as well as volume and line—was given a definite psychological purpose in Greco's best portraits. Above all, this goal of psychological realism was given, when necessary, an undeniable priority—even to the point of deformation—over the physical naturalism of the portrait; a most exceptional achievement, not yet, perhaps, fully appraised.

Indeed, if in this portrait the lavish use of color accents makes the voluminous ruff still more voluminous, still more heavily loaded with some new and rich substance, it is to transform this huge and luminous frame of the face into a living thing that accepts the intrusion of the head's invading outline. And if in the midst of the realistic and simplified modeling of the face a sudden and abnormal asymmetry is introduced in the eyes' position and in the outline of the mouth, this contrast is intended to dramatize more the indelible, perhaps sanguine individuality of the portrayed features.

Hard worker he was, El Greco; this portrait is a living proof of it. With the decisive, yet never final stabs of his brush—the "*crueles borrones*," as Pacheco called them—El Greco used to retouch his canvases ambitiously, unceasingly.

CARDINAL TAVERA

Painted 1609–14
40⅛ × 32⅝"
Hospital of San Juan Bautista, Toledo

There is as much privation in this portrait of a Cardinal-Archbishop, as there is richness in that of the jurist de Cevallos (page 101). El Greco never painted bodies without ideas belonging to them. He painted significations, he painted meanings—and our obligation to feel and respond to them.

Everything is reduced to the very idea of economy in this effigy of a great church dignitary: one erect triangle for the architecture of the figure—and no more; one hand, a beautiful single hand—and no more to it; the crimson of the mantle—crimson, nothing else; and one truth of the face—the skull.

Everything is rigid, motionless, everything, save the living eyes. That is how the dead Cardinal-Archbishop of Toledo, who was also, they say, a good man, came to life.

(This, perhaps the last, portrait by Greco is referred to on page 21 of the Introduction.)

COLORPLATE 29

THE SAVIOUR

Painted 1604–14 (Cossio); 1603–12 (Mayer)
39 × 31"
Greco Museum, Toledo

The Byzantine character of this icon is unmistakable. It is puzzling, in a work of so late and so fully emancipated a period of Greco's activity, to find such typical, if external and conventional, traits of Byzantine art: the facial type, the hieratic gesture, the rigid frontality, the intense fixity of the eyes. Perhaps Greco painted this icon for one of his numerous refugee compatriots in Spain, some of whom were of high rank.

In its other aspects, however, the painting is Greco's to the core. Typical of him are the copper-and-silver luminosity of the green and red; the combination of virile solemnity and feminine delicacy in the features and silhouette of Christ; the contrast between the hand raised in blessing—active and actively delineated as if separated from the rest.of the painting by deep shadows—and the hand that reposes on the globe—passive, feminine, penetrated with and obedient to light.

ADORATION OF THE SHEPHERDS

Painted during the last period (c. 1604–14)
64⅜ × 42⅛"
The Metropolitan Museum of Art, New York

The night came with no surprises to those peaceful men who gathered around the Woman and her Child wrapped in white. With them there were other things and beings: the thickly leaved branches, the good animals, and also a strange open vault—either not yet finished, or already ruined.

Then, suddenly, the young Mother lifted up the linen and the Child appeared to all—a pure and new source of light, a flow of pure white, brushed in rapid strokes upon a bed of gray—Child and linen as luminous as the poor immolated lamb lying on the ground.

Others—Correggio, Raphael—had already painted a similar source of light suddenly illuminating the night all around. El Greco knew it. He exalted not the light but the surprise of it. A great shudder runs through the entire group to the left and the group thus becomes one composite, surprised body, thrown vertically and made of several bodies emerging from and completing each other. And what surprise in the sudden opening of the old man's arms and hands (to the right), before even his staff, devoid of support and balance, had started to fall! What surprise also in the flickering light that reaches the limbs of the kneeling man and, transformed there into flames—orange, green—transforms in its turn these limbs into pure rhythms!

But El Greco did not stop here: for it is the very transmission of this event and of this surprise that he wanted to tell us. Throughout the zigzagging progression of now clasped, now opened and lifted hands, and thence to the descending dance of the cherubs, the good tidings were transmitted away back to the formidable standing figure, and into the formidable distance. The threatening light that descends from the apocalyptic sky there, is it the transmitted light of the good tidings or is it a different, a menacing new light?

VIEW AND PLAN OF TOLEDO

Painted 1604–14 (Cossío); c. 1609 (Mayer)
53⅛ × 89¾"
Greco Museum, Toledo

First impression: a certain feeling of chaos. A swarming of inhabited stones, houses, streets, walls, that climb toward the top of the steep hill and, in reaching it, spread out, exhibiting against the cloudy sky their shaggy profile—shaggy uncombed hair on a half-bald skull. The arbitrary presence of the ocher earth, allegorical figure of the River Tagus to the left in the foreground, and to the right of the sad-looking youth, possibly Greco's son, presenting to us the plan of the city. The arbitrarily isolated building supported by a cloud. The sky group of the Virgin bringing to St. Ildefonso, Toledo's patron, the legendary chasuble.

But, says the immediately overlapping second impression, are not the two side figures, Tagus and the youth, like the two ends of a bow's arch, the arch of the city's silhouette, suggesting a rather well-organized composition, where everything seems to converge toward the central object of our attention—the huge map?

Yet, adds instantly the third impression, everything here is shown to us in a manner that emphasizes the isolation of images from each other.

Let us turn then, we say to ourselves, to the central and isolated object, the map: El Greco's intention must surely be located there. It contains a written document, a long inscription:

„It has been necessary to put the hospital of Don Juan Tavera in the form of a model (that on the cloud) because it is not only so happened as to conceal the Visagra gate, but thrust up to its dome or cupola in such a manner that it over-topped the town; once put thus as a model, and removed from its place, I thought it would show the façade before any other part of it; how the rest of it is related to the town will be seen on the map.

"Also, in the story of Our Lady who brings the chasuble to St. Ildefonso for his embellishment, so as to enlarge the figures, I have availed myself, to a certain extent, of their being heavenly bodies, in the same way as lights, seen from afar, appear large, however small they be." (Robert Byron's translation.)

The painting is a kind of geographical-statistical document; but—and here is El Greco at his deepest—he gave life to lifeless things in the picture: he made the sculptured figure of the river a living, if bizarre, human being; he temporarily banished life's intensity from the limbs of youth and gave it to the inanimate map; he made the escutcheon in the sky a living thing, nailed to a real sky.

COLORPLATE 32

TOLEDO

Painted 1604–14 (Cossio)
47¾ × 42¾"
The Metropolitan Museum of Art, New York

Never has such a landscape been painted. And yet all the simplest and usual elements of a landscape painting are there: sky, hills, a city, the deep gorge of a river, trees, meadows, roads. But the main thing is missing: the feeling of space, of distance. Dominant, instead, is what in painting is usually conveyed by the human figure only: the feeling of activity, of drama. The sky is rent catastrophically in a chaotic rush of its clouds; while the earth dashes to meet it in an upward surge. The movement of the hilly roads, now crossing each other, now separating, forms a curious ornamental and active pattern of interlaced triangles. There is a strange rearrangement of the topography of Toledo: the Cathedral placed on the wrong side of the Castle; the imaginary city gate with trees; the changed architecture of the towers of Alcantara bridge. The city is presented both full-face (buildings showing their façades) and in profile (their accentuated flattening), and there is a subtle contrast between this flatness—including the ornamental flight of the roads—and the bulging of the great clouds, swelled with heaven's lightings, heaven's wrath and heaven's blue.

This menacing anger is accumulated—its symbolic darkness is thickened— behind the zone of Toledo's most conspicuous and haughty buildings: the Cathedral and the Castle, the Alcazar. The threatening dark wrath of the sky points to the stormy embodiment of the joint powers of the city: the power of the Church and the power of the State. Indeed, why is it that the colors of the sky's wrath are absent from the earth? And why so peaceful and indifferent to the storm the activity of all these people, microscopic, needle-like people, scattered among the green, walking toward the gate of the city or busy on the bank of the Tagus? Why, if not to tell us the peace of all that is detached from the menacing city, that does not belong to it?

Did El Greco tell us here, in this reconstructed image of Toledo, his own myth and his own judgment of the nearest-to-heaven powers of earth? Is this a mysterious portrait of the inner man's crime of power, with punishment—and redemption—in it?

CHRIST ON THE MOUNT OF OLIVES

Painted during the last period
40⅛ × 52"
National Gallery, London

This may be an *atelier* work; yet, on the whole, in its expressiveness and revelation, it is as integrally El Greco's as the version accepted as from his own hand. It belongs to the painter's last period of exulting liberation. Indeed, if Christ's figure orders the rhythm and the delineation of the glassy rock behind it, this plastic echoing is not simply obedience here; it is the expression of active sympathy with Christ's tragic solitude.

Nowhere else had El Greco used more freely and with more psychological originality of narration the medieval symbolical principle of continuity and interpenetration of forms. And nowhere, perhaps, had his color organization acquired such a degree of expressiveness as here: contrasts of cool, isolated pink, yellow, green, blue, violet, brown, gray tones; and at the same time, the impressive nearness of dark and light tone values makes colored shadows seem like accented lights, and lights seem like exalted shadows.

That is how the story is told of Christ's last prayer before the chalice of bitterest decision and destiny was brought to him by the angel. Christ is on watch; His Disciples are in profound sleep. And the angel appearing to Christ seems also to involve the sleepers in his bodily presence. Watch and sleep become one event; one reality. The three sleeping figures are enclosed, involved in their own rhythm, and this rhythm is continued in the radiating ornamental rhythm of the rocks. And wave against wave, the figure of Christ is opened, spread out; Christ's spreading arms, Christ's spreading folds! Wave against wave, yet all meet in one great wave.

But behind this marvelous reality—all light, fullness, nearness—another dream of reality is preparing its invasion: the apocalyptic lunar distance, with the terror of soldiers in it. Greco's liberty is unshaken, but the world at large is not.

CHRIST ON THE MOUNT OF OLIVES
(detail)

Painted during the last period
National Gallery, London

Most strikingly here and in the upper part of the *Burial of Count Orgaz* (page 37), with which this detail has affinities strange for so late a production of El Greco, there is a medieval sense of the continuity of forms and rhythms. This mobile continuity is expressed by the strong spiraling movement which begins with the sharp-edged hem of the angel's robe and follows around the mouth of the cave which encloses the sleeping Apostles. In the upper part of this detail the spiraling movement, counterpointed by dark areas of sky, involves the clouds and the angel's half-spread wings.

What makes this detail so fascinating is the co-existence of this continuity with a rigid stability and bareness of forms. Rigidity is evident in the metallic and stiffly silhouetted robe of the angel, in the gaunt branch, and in the rigidly geometric folds of the Apostles' robes. The opposition of the metallic greenish yellow and grayish blue is unmodulated.

The co-existence of continuity and isolation suggests the duality of the total painting: the unawareness of the sleeping Apostles, the preparation of Christ for the sacrifice.

There is a curious detail of perspective in the fact that the branch, which is nearer to us than the angel, is at one point obscured by the angel's robe. This rearrangement of perspective suggests the spatial liberation of the celestial figure.

CHRIST ON THE MOUNT OF OLIVES
(detail)

Painted during the last period
National Gallery, London

Around the solitude and abandonment of Christ's figure is poured the consolation of sympathy and solidarity. The emphasis here is on the warmth of the colors: the pink-red blends with the greenish-brown of the soil and the rock; the blue and the red of Christ's robes are united by the continuity of high lights. This harmonized warmth of coloring seems to envelop and perhaps protect the kneeling Christ.

Like the colors, the rock behind, its shape echoing and almost enveloping His form, seems a gesture of nature's protection. But the rock is not massive or impenetrable: cloaklike, glassy, malleable, as fragile in its illusion as a scenic flat, it expresses the sympathy between Christ and the surrounding world, but at the same time that it separates Him from the other figures, it is insufficient to protect Him from the tragedy.

DESCENT OF THE HOLY GHOST

Painted 1607–14 (Cossio); 1603–6 (Mayer)
108⅝ × 50″
The Prado Museum, Madrid

If you look at the tongues of flame you will understand the flames of the hands. If you look at the flames of the hands you will understand the torment and the storm of the bodies. You will understand better the presence of the triangles—the triangles of the bodies' interrelation—which flatten the tormented space and appease it. If you look at this geometrical armature of the flattened space, and remember the Byzantine ancestry of El Greco, you will see and understand another and deeper space structure there. You will see the concave hemisphere of the upper half of the compact scene joining the lower, convex one. You will see the two then forming together a new and curved, egg-shaped perspective: the interior, the cavity, of a space vessel (the ellipse of its edge traced by the hands of the side figures and the two great figures turned backward in the foreground), a vessel in which the floating Dove will be received and guarded.

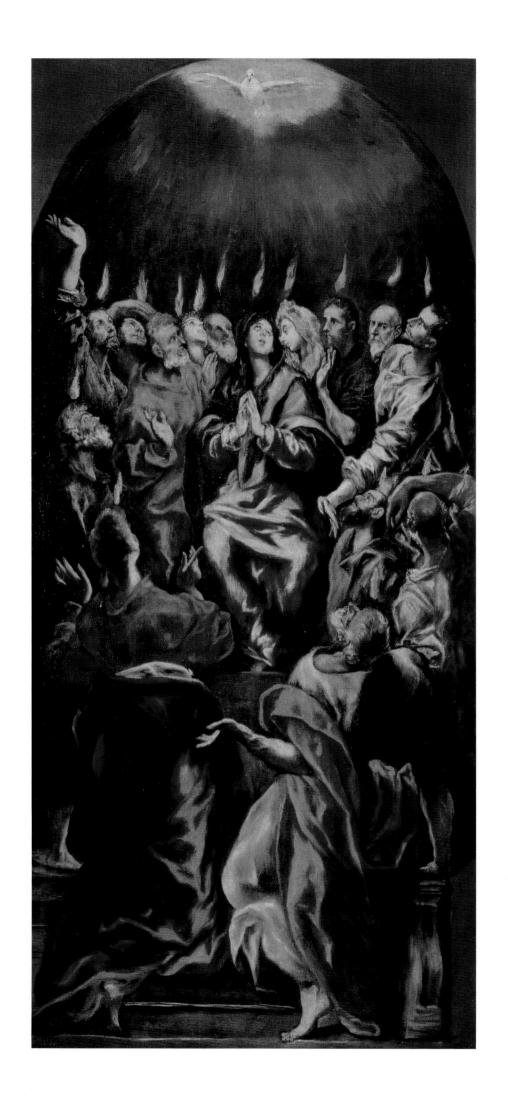

LAOCOÖN

Painted 1604–14 (Cossio); c. 1606–10 (Mayer)
55⅞ × 76"
National Gallery of Art, Washington, D.C. (Kress Collection)

Swift and terrible was the punishment of Laocoön, a priest of Apollo at Troy, and his two sons. According to legend, he had profaned the temple of the god; and additionally, he had incurred the wrath of Athene for having warned the Trojans against the wooden horse. The famous and so influential marble group of late antiquity, unearthed in 1506, portrays the priest and his sons in their futile struggle with the serpents sent to destroy them. But while the sculpture expresses a community of punishment, El Greco, in painting this subject, wished rather to express the isolation, the individual responsibility, of the three victims.

Each of the figures struggles with his destiny in his own isolated way, without regard or pity for the others. We do not know whether the fallen youth is mortally wounded by the serpent, or already dead. And the other son, upright and interrogating the cloud-loaded sky, may have escaped—in this version of Greco's—the serpent's venom, as he has already escaped the expressively feeble coils. (This liberation, it is true, had been suggested in the oldest version of the legend, by Arctinus of Miletus, and was remembered later by Goethe in his commentary on the Rhodian marble.)

Greco's fallen and struggling Laocoön, more fascinated than terrified, his eyes against the serpent's fangs, seems also to be free from its coils. Will the benevolent witnessing—always the witnessing in Greco's art!—of the scene by the two punishing gods, Apollo and Artemis, assure his final triumph?

The equivocal reigns here. The legs of Apollo are feminine and those of Artemis masculine. The city of Toledo is portrayed here, open to the Trojan horse, to certain doom: did Greco choose to do this out of love, or wrath, or hatred?

In the subject matter and treatment—elliptical, planes and contours an interrelation of curves and angles—everything is centrifugal, separated, capsizing. And yet an ardent unity permeates the whole painting: the two divinities joining heaven and earth; the upright buttressing figures at both sides of the painting; the unity of the brown-gray-greenish color action. . . .

THE VISION OF ST. JOHN

Painted 1604–14 (Cossio)
87½ × 76"
The Metropolitan Museum of Art, New York

Discovered by the Spanish painter, Ignacio Zuloaga, behind an old velvet curtain in Cordoba, this picture was at first called—and is still called by some—*Sacred and Profane Love*. M. Cossio calls this an "inexplicable and arbitrary title." He suggested—and the consensus of authorities now make this suggestion definitive —the Apocalyptic subject of the Opening of the Fifth Seal, with the image of the Lamb among the Four Symbols, for a missing upper part. The text of Revelation 6:9–11, part of which was indicated by M. Cossio, should be considered in its entirety:

"9. And when he [the Lamb] had opened the fifth seal, I saw under the altar the souls of them that were slain for the word of God, and for the testimony which they held:

"10. And they cried with a loud voice, saying, How long, O Lord, holy and true, dost thou not judge and avenge our blood on them that dwell on the earth?

"11. And white robes were given unto every one of them; and it was said unto them, that they should rest yet for a little season, until their fellowservants also and their brethren, that should be killed as they were, should be fulfilled."

Apocalyptic garments cling to the resuscitated bodies, but they are not the "white robes" only; what is the meaning of this unexpected addition of amber and green robes? Professor Meyer Schapiro has suggested to me that El Greco perhaps follows the Old French gloss in the Apocalypse MSS, where it is said that the white robe is given to the martyred saints to signify that their souls and bodies are in the earth and they see Christ in the glorified flesh; their cry is for the Last Judgment and the resurrection of their bodies, when they will receive "another robe" and be above the altar; that is, they will have a full knowledge of the Christ's divinity, and their glory will be doubled, for they will be glorified in body and soul. If this gloss is pertinent, here, it would appear to mean that El Greco had represented not only the opening of the fifth seal, but also its interpretation as a prophecy of the Last Judgment; hence the figures rising from the ground as in images of the Last Judgment.

COLORPLATE 39

BAPTISM OF CHRIST

Painted c. 1609–14 (Cossío)
162¼ × 76¾"
Hospital of San Juan Bautista, Toledo

Earth and heaven are joined finally. That, which in *Orgaz* (page 63) was only earth's and heaven's proximity, a bold and closest possible proximity it is true; that, which later—in the *Descent of the Holy Ghost* (page 119)—was given as heaven's descent into earth's womb, or—in *The Vision of St. John* (page 123)—as earth's prophetic and scaling leap toward heaven, became here finally a total and inextricable union of the two worlds.

The *Baptism* is both the fulfillment of this union (at the point of junction from which the golden path of the Holy Dove descends) and the announcement of it. Besides this, nothing else is left in the new universe created by Greco.

The bound-together, interrelated forms of the whole picture: the waters of the Baptism becoming the very substance of this united, compact world—a deep, undulating and deforming, green-and-yellow substance; the mysterious colloquy between the eyes of Christ and the eyes of the angel in front of Him; the heaven-reaching hand of the green angel (so often painted by Greco in his later period, with the same enigmatic gesture and the same emphasis on the figure's elongation)—everything here is the Baptism of fulfillment and announcement.

124

COLORPLATE 40

ASSUMPTION OF THE VIRGIN

Painted 1608–13 (Cossio)

127½ × 65¾″

Museum of San Vicente, Toledo

There are no Apostles here to watch and to share the miracle, nor is there a sepulcher as evidence of the event. The absence of these and other conventional attributes of an Assumption accounts for the varying interpretations of the picture: to some authorities this is an Immaculate Conception. But whatever the merits, from an iconographical view, of the alternative readings, the pictorial quality of the scene is clear—the holy figure ascends amidst a chorus of angels. A spray of roses and lilies, alien to the disappearing, low earth, represents all that the Virgin's body had been. The sinuous fullness of the entire figure complex of the picture is anticipated in the fullness of this spray of flowers.

The Virgin's Assumption is not the emerging or self-levitation of a body: Her body is a continuation of the being of the larger-winged angel. Her Assumption is an assumption of everything in the painting, including the fiery and waning heaven in which her transfigured head plunges. It is a perpetual Assumption: *"mas alto!"*—"higher!"—and the goal is one never to be reached. This is El Greco's ultimate vision, a vision of a perpetually ascending, spiraling, divine world, of sion its fullness in everlasting self-transformation or change.

The illusion of depth—the eye's familiar horizontal depth of space has become here a vertical depth. The Virgin's blue mantle may be the real axis—a whirlwind-like axis—about which all other forms are constructed; yet the vibrancy of this blue, the scattering of blue around and outside it, shifts this axis to centers of red, yellow, or gray. As in the suspended feet of the angel to the left, the ascension of bodies has become a quiet floating.

The universe is both static and mobile here: a full universe. Color, light, volume, linearity—all become one pictorial substance in which figure and milieu adhere to each other, penetrate into each other, and shape each other's reality.